'Meet Shadow'
the
Siberian Husky

By Rebecca Macniven

ISBN- 13: 978-1503097537
ISBN-10: 1503097536

CONTENTS

This is Shadow

He is a Siberian husky

Shadow lives in England with his family who love him lots. This book will teach you all about Shadow, how we care for him, what he eats and what he likes to do.

Shadow needs a lot of sleep, being a puppy means he is growing fast so he gets tired easily.
He likes to sleep on a soft rug because it is like cuddling his mummy.
When he wakes up he is ready to play and eat again, Shadow is just like a human baby.

Training

It is important for you to train your puppy so that he has respect for you and knows he must listen to you. This means that you can keep him and others around him safe.

If he knows that you are the boss he will always do what you ask him to do.

"If you are a good owner you will have a good dog".

Shadows safety is important to us so we teach him to sit at the road side when we need to cross so he doesn't get run over.

We teach him to wait when we give him a treat so he will only take it when we say he can, he knows to be gentle so he doesn't hurt our fingers.

He knows not to jump up at people because his claws could scratch them or he might knock them over.

Shadow can do a few other tricks like: give paw, high five or lay down, he even gives a kiss.

Here is Shadow with his owner Lewis. They are best friends and spend a lot of time together. The important rule, that Shadow knows, is that Lewis is the boss.
Lewis does not shout at Shadow or hit him. He teaches him to do the right things by telling him he is a "good boy". He gives him a treat when he is good. He will tell him "BAD" if he is naughty and tell him to "SIT".

You know when a puppy is happy because he smiles at you and wags his tail. Can you see Shadow's smile? He is happy because he has been for a nice long walk and played with his owner. Shadow loves Lewis because he gives him everything he needs; food, water, love, cuddles, walks, training and friendship.

Walking

Having a dog is a big responsibility, you will have to walk him every day for the rest of his life, make sure he has fresh food and water, a warm place to sleep, lots of playing and attention.

You need to teach your dog how to be friends with other dogs and people. Dogs are very sociable, they love to have company.

Shadow goes out for a long walk before and after school. He wears this harness so his lead doesn't pull on his collar. This teaches him not to pull when he is walking with his lead on. The harness is nice and strong so he can't break it. A long walk is good because it burns his extra energy.

"A tired dog is a happy dog".

We like to make sure that Shadow gets lots of time to play and explore because it makes him feel happy and satisfied.

Different dogs like to play and discover things in different ways. Some like to sniff about or chase balls, others like to play with their friends or dig holes.

Most Huskies are quite loving and very pretty but they are also bred to pull sledges and hunt for their food, it is important to remember this.

Even if they don't need to pull or hunt it is in their nature to do it anyway so their instincts will usually take over.

If Shadow sees any little animals like squirrels or birds he naturally wants to chase them. Just like a Collie dog enjoys rounding up sheep, or a beagle loves to sniff and find things.

Because of this we have to be careful where we can let Shadow run around without his lead on. He may run into trouble. When a Husky starts to chase and run they can go on for a long time.

Feeding

All big dogs need to have their food and water bowls raised up off the ground. This is so that they don't have to bend down to eat or drink. This special bowl stand can be made higher or lower. As Shadow grows bigger we can lift his bowls higher.

Shadow eats the best dry puppy food and has water available all day so he can eat and drink if he feels hungry or thirsty. We make sure Shadow doesn't eat too much or he will be sick and won't be a happy puppy. Good quality food makes him healthy so he doesn't gain too much weight.

Grooming

Shadow needs to be groomed regularly because he sheds his fur twice a year. This means that some of his fur falls out to make room for a new coat, which is better suited to the weather. He has two coats; a topcoat and an undercoat to keep him super warm in the cold weather.

Shadow has a lot fur. When it is ready to fall out it goes everywhere. When we brush him, it feels like it is never going to stop coming out. We help to loosen the fur more by giving him a nice warm bath. We wash him with puppy shampoo and rinse him well. This makes brushing him much easier. He shakes himself off making everything soaking wet. Then we use a towel to dry him, ready for a big long brush.

These are the brushes that we use to groom Shadow's fur.
The blue one is called a de-shedding brush and the yellow one is a de-shedding comb.
Shadow doesn't really like being brushed so we have to be really kind and gentle. We give him some treats for being good while we brush him.

Shadow would get very hot in the summer if he didn't loose his thick undercoat.

In the winter the thick warm undercoat grows back again. This keeps him really warm so he can stay out in the snowy weather and not feel cold.

All year round his topcoat works as a waterproof layer, a bit like a raincoat. This helps to keep his skin dry and warm.

In the summer Shadow's topcoat is like a sun block. This stops him from getting too hot.

Look how much fur comes out when we brush him. The bigger Shadow gets the more fur he has.

Q. How long do you think it might take to brush all this fur out of Shadow?

A. It takes more than an hour of brushing to get all this fur out of Shadow!

Digging

Huskies love to dig. We are lucky because we have a big field where all the dogs can play near our home. The field is a place where the dogs can run, play, chase each other and dig. This is where Shadow is allowed to dig as much as he wants. Shadow has really good hearing. He listens carefully to the little creatures underground and then pounces.

Shadow's Friends.

Shadow has lots of doggy friends which he meets up with regularly so he can play with them. Shadow loves to play with his friends.

Dogs make new friends by sniffing the special scent gland that is at the bottom of their tails. You can tell when dogs like one another because they wag their tails to say "Lets Play" and they do a special play bow. If they are not sure whether they like the other dog they might get scared and run away, growl or show their teeth.

Playtime

These are some of Shadow's favorite toys. It is important for him to have playtime inside the house as well as outside. Dogs can get bored just like you and I. Shadow has fun playing with his toys. Having his own toys stops him from chewing things he shouldn't!

Leaving Shadow alone

If we go out we can't be too long, Shadow can get lonely easily. We hide little dog biscuits in his treat toy for him to find. This activity keeps Shadow entertained.

Can you see how Shadow moves the pieces with his mouth? He also uses his nose and his paws to slide the shapes out of the way and get to his treats.

What a clever boy!

Shadow is happy when he gets....

plenty of sleep....

Lots of exercise....

Somewhere safe and warm with love, food, water, plenty of toys, cuddles and attention.

What more could a puppy want?

Dedication

The inspiration for this book came mainly from my son
Lewis and Shadow our husky.
Lewis, I would like you to know that a life without you in it
would be quite boring and I treasure every second I get to
be with you.

I would also like to thank my sister
Rachel Macniven for her contribution of the stunning cover
photo.

There is also a group of friends who have spent their
valuable time helping me compile and edit my first book,
thanks for all your support and belief in me.
Particular thanks to Alix, you have been my rock through
the highs and lows, I owe you so much.

Much love to you all.

Don't go!

If you enjoyed this book you can keep up with shadow daily on his facebook page or on his blog page.
You can see photos and videos of what he is getting up to and you can keep up to date with new and future book releases, which follow this one.

You can message Shadow and ask any questions you like or if you have any suggestions for future books I will happily listen to your ideas.

Please ask permission from a guardian before using the internet.

http://shadowthesiberianhusky.wordpress.com

https://www.facebook.com/siberianhuskyshadow

email: shadowthehusky@live.com

Printed in Great Britain
by Amazon